MW01284963

Frog Kids Colo
+Fun Facts about Frog & Toad

Children Activity Book for Boys & Girls Age 3-8,
with 30 Super Fun Coloring Pages of Frogs,
The Prince-in-Disguise Animal, in Lots of Fun Actions!

Copyright © 2016 by Jackie D. Fluffy

The average age of a frog or a toad is between 4 and 15 years; however, some frogs can live up to 40 years!

A group of frogs is called an
ARMY of frogs.

A group of toads is called a
KNOT of toads.

Some frogs and toads can change their colors, such as the Gray Tree Frogs in the United States which usually change their colors from bright green to gray.

Actually most frogs and toads have lungs with which they can breathe; however, mostly they breathe through their skin.

Frogs can hear by the big round ears
on the sides of their head.

Frog is pretty common character in fairy tale, especially Frog prince, the well known fairy tale from collection of brothers Grimm.

Some frogs can throw up their entire stomach then wipe it off with their legs, if they happen to eat something toxic.

Tongue of a frog's can be flipped out so accurately and rapidly, because it is how they catch an insect and other food.

Toads can live farther from water
sources than frogs can,
because a toad's skin does not dry out
as fast as a frog's skin would do.

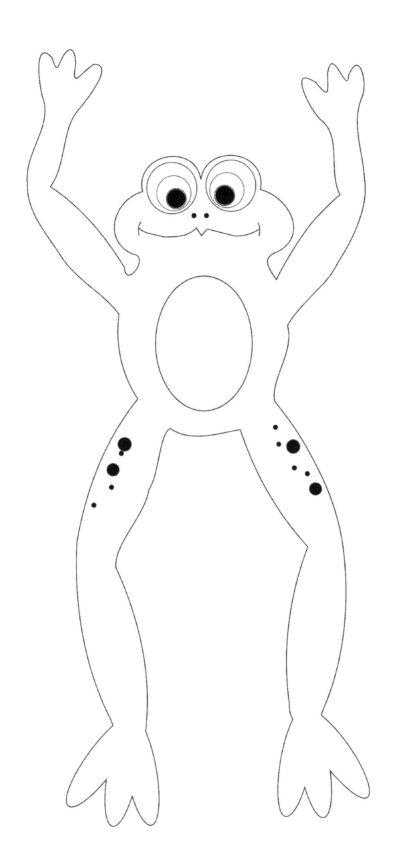

The largest frog in the world is
the Goliath Frog in Africa,
which can weigh even more than 7 pounds!

The smallest frog in the world is
the Eleutherodactylus iberia frog in Cuba,
which is only 1 cm. (0.39 inch) long!

Main habitat of frogs is in or near ponds.

A frog completely sheds its skin
about once a week,
and then eats its own old skin.

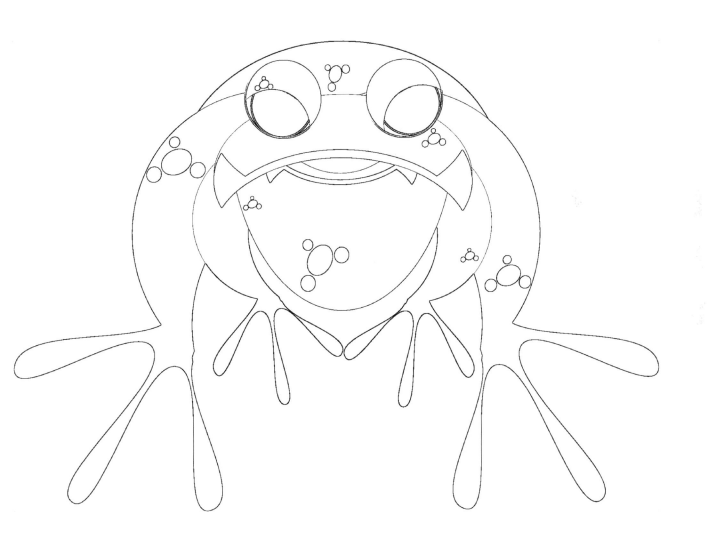

The glass frog has translucent skin.
We can see its internal organs working,
including the heart beating,
through its skin.

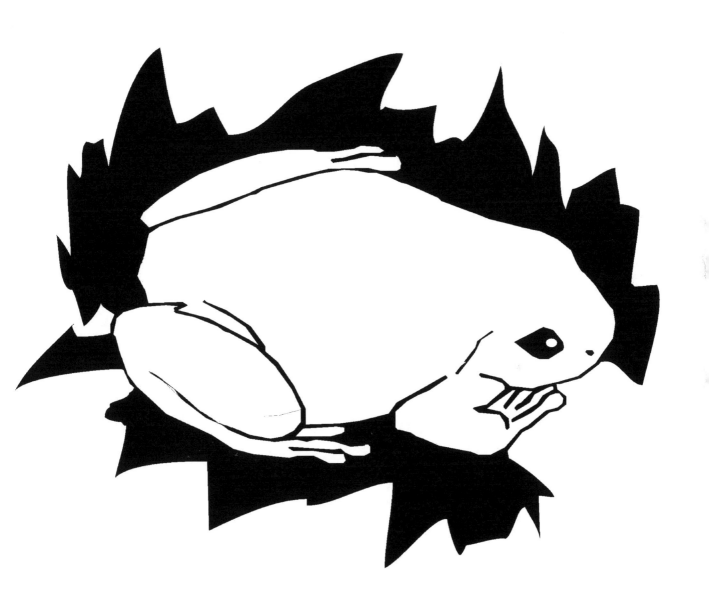

Most frogs actually have teeth.
They use their teeth to hold prey in place
before swallowing it.

Frogs and toads are amphibian, which means they live both on land and in water.

Frogs and toads will die if their skin dries out, so they have to live near a damp place like ponds or swamps.

Instead of drinking like we do, frogs consume water by soaking it into their body through their skin!

Frogs are everywhere! We can find frogs and toads in almost every climate and all over the world, except only for Antarctica.

A frog named Darwin's frog was named after Charles Darwin who discovered it on his world voyage.

A frog named the ornate horned frog is the most aggressive frog. When felt threatened, they will jump toward their enemy and bite them!

Frogs are so good at jumping.
Some frogs can jump over 20 times their
own body length, which is comparable to a
man jumping 30m. (98 ft.) !

Frogs lay their eggs in water.
The eggs hatch into a tadpole,
which lives in water for some time,
until it grows up and become an adult frog.

Asian tree frogs build nests in trees above water. When the tadpoles hatch, they fall directly into the water.

In Egypt the frog is the symbol of life and fertility.

Frogs hibernate in the wintertime.

Not all frogs are green.
Some are red and some are yellow and
some are brown. They have different
patterns on their skins too.

We can easily tell a male frog from a female frog by checking out its ears. A male has its ear as big as its eyes, while a female has her ear smaller than her eyes.

The male frog is the only one who can croak.

Hi there!
It's me, Jackie D. Fluffy!
I hope you like this book like I do.
What's the next animal you want to color??
Let me know by writing a review on

www.amazon.com

Sure! It will be fun and useful!
With much thanks and love,
Jackie D. Fluffy

Made in the USA
San Bernardino, CA
26 July 2016